AN INTRODUCTION TO THE PARABLES
THROUGH PROGRAMMED INSTRUCTION

WILLIAM RICHARD STEGNER

University Press of America™

Copyright © 1977 by

University Press of America™

division of
R.F. Publishing, Inc.
4710 Auth Place, S.E., Washington, D.C. 20023

All rights reserved

Printed in the United States of America

0-8191-0132-x

This program has been designed for college and seminary students whose verbal aptitudes range from 450 to 800 on the scale of the SAT.

High scores on the test on this unit have been achieved by students who devoted two to five hours to the program, the amount of time necessary being in proportion to verbal aptitudes.

The following pages offer you a *methodical way of learning*. Do not treat the project as a test. You are not to hurry. Move along only when you feel that you have absorbed the information in each frame.

After you learn to recognize the characteristics of an allegory and how to find its meaning, you will work with the characteristics of the parable as a literary form that is found in the New Testament. Then you will be taught the principle of interpretation by which you may discover the meaning of most of the New Testament parables. Opportunities will be provided for you to develop skill in using this principle of interpretation by applying it to several parables.

Be sure to perform the tasks (check, draw lines, underline, etc.) assigned to you in each frame. Since you will wish to check your responses you can consult answers given either on the same page, or on the page following.

Having completed the unit, you should be able to:

a. recognize many of the New Testament parables since you will be working directly with passages from the New Testament.
b. recognize the characteristics of the parables as a literary form.
c. develop experience in finding the meaning of a given parable.

When you are ready, turn the page and start.

Parables

Start here   Frame # 1

Instructions here: In this space you will be told what to look for in the material given below.

Examine the parable below to determine whether Jesus observed nature or understood natural processes.

Often a quotation or parable here:

And he said, "With what can we compare the kingdom of God, or what parable shall we use for it? It is like a grain of mustard seed, which, when sown upon the ground, is the smallest of all the seeds on earth; yet when it is sown it grows up and becomes the greatest of all shrubs, and puts forth large branches, so that the birds of the air can make nests in its shade." Mark 4:30-32

Some tasks set for you:

Underline the alternative in the sentence below that accurately describes the above parable.

　　The parable reveals a knowledge of the (agricultural practices)
　　(urban conditions) of the time.

Now you check the answers either found on the next page or given at the bottom of this page, as is true in this case.

ANSWER to Frame # 1

　　The parable reveals a knowledge of the (<u>agricultural practices</u>)
　　(urban conditions) of the time.

Having compared your answer with the answer on this page, go to the next frame. ⟶

The next four frames are designed to show the range of observations about life that Jesus makes in the parables.

Parables

Exhibit for Frame # 2

Instructions for the use of this exhibit will be found on the opposite page.

I. And he said to them, "Which of you who has a friend will go to him at midnight and say to him, 'Friend, lend me three loaves; for a friend of mine has arrived on a journey, and I have nothing to set before him'; and he will answer from within, 'Do not bother me; the door is now shut, and my children are with me in bed; I cannot get up and give you anything'? I tell you, though he will not get up and give him anything because he is his friend, yet because of his importunity he will rise and give him whatever he needs." Luke 11:5-8

II. He also said to the disciples, "There was a rich man who had a steward, and charges were brought to him that this man was wasting his goods. And he called him and said to him, 'What is this that I hear about you? Turn in the account of your stewardship, for you can no longer be steward.' And the steward said to himself, 'What shall I do, since my master is taking the stewardship away from me? I am not strong enough to dig, and I am ashamed to beg. I have decided what to do, so that people may receive me into their houses when I am put out of the stewardship.' So, summoning his master's debtors one by one, he said to the first, 'How much do you owe my master?' He said, 'A hundred measures of oil.' And he said to him, 'Take your bill, and sit down quickly and write fifty.' Then he said to another, 'And how much do you owe?' He said, 'A hundred measures of wheat.' He said to him, 'Take your bill, and write eighty.' The master commended the dishonest steward for his prudence; for the sons of this world are wiser in their own generation than the sons of light." Luke 16:1-8

III. And he told them a parable, to the effect that they ought always to pray and not lose heart. He said, "In a certain city there was a judge who neither feared God nor regarded man; and there was a widow in that city who kept coming to him and saying, 'Vindicate me against my adversary.' For a while he refused; but afterward he said to himself, 'Though I neither fear God nor regard man, yet because this widow bothers me, I will vindicate her, or she will wear me out by her continual coming.'" And the Lord said, "Hear what the unrighteous judge says. And will not God vindicate his elect, who cry to him day and night? Will he delay long over them? I tell you, he will vindicate them speedily." Luke 18:1-8

Parables

Frame # 2

Read the parables in the exhibit on the opposite page to determine how Jesus portrayed human life in these parables.

Draw a circle around the letter of the statements (below) that make correct observations about the parables on the opposite page.

    a. The man within the house did a favor for his friend out of pure kindness.

    b. The man within the house did a favor to save himself further trouble.

    c. The steward put self-interest above honesty and profited from his shrewdness and lack of principle.

    d. The steward tried to minimize his employer's losses in a shrinking market that pointed to a coming depression.

    e. The judge answered the widow's request because he was tired of her constant nagging and wanted to be left in peace.

    f. The judge answered the widow's request because he wanted to be known as an upright and civic-minded citizen.

    g. In these parables Jesus is drawing an ideal picture, showing life as it ought to be lived.

    h. In these parables Jesus is observing what life is like and picturing the real world in his teaching.

ANSWER to Frame # 2

b.   c.   e.   h.

Parables

Exhibit for Frame # 3

I. "For it will be as when a man going on a journey called his servants and entrusted to them his property; to one he gave five talents, to another two, to another one, to each according to his ability. Then he went away. He who had received the five talents went at once and traded with them; and he made five talents more. So too, he who had the two talents made two talents more. But he who had received the one talent, went and dug in the ground and hid his master's money. Now after a long time the master of those servants came and settled accounts with them. And he who had received the five talents came forward, bringing five talents more, saying, 'Master, you delivered to me five talents; here I have made five talents more.' His master said to him, 'Well done, good and faithful servant; you have been faithful over a little, I will set you over much; enter into the joy of your master.' And he also who had the two talents came forward, saying, 'Master, you delivered to me two talents; here I have made two talents more.' His master said to him, 'Well done, good and faithful servant; you have been faithful over a little, I will set you over much; enter into the joy of your master.' He also who had received the one talent came forward, saying, 'Master, I knew you to be a hard man, reaping where you did not sow, and gathering where you did not winnow; so I was afraid, and I went and hid your talent in the ground. Here you have what is yours.' But his master answered him, 'You wicked and slothful servant! You knew that I reap where I have not sowed, and gather where I have not winnowed? Then you ought to have invested my money with the bankers, and at my coming I should have received what was my own with interest. So take the talent from him, and give it to him who has the ten talents." Matthew 25:14-28

II. And the Lord said, "Who then is the faithful and wise steward, whom his master will set over his household, to give them their portion of food at the proper time? Blessed is that servant whom his master when he comes will find so doing. Truly I tell you, he will set him over all his possessions. But if that servant says to himself, 'My master is delayed in coming,' and begins to beat the menservants and the maidservants, and to eat and drink and get drunk, the master of that servant will come on a day when he does not expect him and at an hour he does not know, and will punish him, and put him with the unfaithful." Luke 12:42-46

III. "Take heed, watch; for you do not know when the time will come. It is like a man going on a journey, when he leaves home and puts his servants in charge, each with his work, and commands the doorkeeper to be on the watch. Watch therefore - for you do not know when the master of the house will come, in the evening, or at midnight, or at cockcrow, or in the morning - lest he come suddenly and find you asleep. And what I say to you I say to all: Watch." Mark 13:33-37

Parables

Frame # 3

Study the parables given in the exhibit on the opposite page to determine Jesus's insight into the relationship between masters and servants.

A list of statements about the parables in the exhibit are given below. Circle the letter "T" when a correct statement is made about the parables and the letter "F" when a false statement is made about the parables.

T   F   a. The servants are waiting for the masters to return.

T   F   b. The parables seem to be addressing a warning to some group.

T   F   c. In ancient times some masters entrusted great responsibility to some of their servants.

T   F   d. There was no need for servants to fear their masters because masters could not punish their servants and slaves.

T   F   e. The servants pictured in these parables are not typical because servants do not take advantage of their master's absence. Hence, the exhortations to faithfulness are not needed.

T   F   f. According to these parables Jesus showed genuine sensitivity to the relationships that existed between servants and their masters.

ANSWER to Frame # 3

(T)   F   a. The servants are waiting for the masters to return.

(T)   F   b. The parables seem to be addressing a warning to some group.

(T)   F   c. In ancient times some masters entrusted great responsibility to some of their servants.

T   (F)   d. There was no need for servants to fear their masters because masters could not punish their servants and slaves.

T   (F)   e. The servants pictured in these parables are not typical because servants do not take advantage of their master's absence. Hence, the exhortations to faithfulness are not needed.

(T)   F   f. According to these parables Jesus showed genuine sensitivity to the relationships that existed between servants and their masters.

Parables

Exhibit for Frame # 4

A. "What do you think? A man had two sons; and he went to the first and said, 'Son, go and work in the vineyard today.' And he answered, 'I will not'; but afterward he repented and went. And he went to the second and said the same; and he answered, 'I go, sir,' but did not go. Which of the two did the will of his father?" They said, "The first." Jesus said to them, "Truly, I say to you, the tax collectors and the harlots go into the kingdom of God before you." Matthew 21:28-31

B. And he said, "There was a man who had two sons; and the younger of them said to his father, 'Father, give me the share of property that falls to me.' And he divided his living between them. Not many days later, the younger son gathered all he had and took his journey into a far country, and there he squandered his property in loose living. And when he had spent everything, a great famine arose in that country, and he began to be in want. So he went and joined himself to one of the citizens of that country, who sent him into his fields to feed swine. And he would gladly have fed on the pods that the swine ate; and no one gave him anything. But when he came to himself he said, 'How many of my father's hired servants have bread enough and to spare, but I perish here with hunger! I will arise and go to my father, and I will say to him, "Father, I have sinned against heaven and before you; I am no longer worthy to be called your son; treat me as one of your hired servants."' And he arose and came to his father. But while he was yet at a distance, his father saw him and had compassion, and ran and embraced him and kissed him. And the son said to him, 'Father, I have sinned against heaven and before you; I am no longer worthy to be called your son.' But the father said to his servants, 'Bring quickly the best robe, and put it on him; and put a ring on his hand, and shoes on his feet; and bring the fatted calf and kill it, and let us eat and make merry; for this my son was dead, and is alive again; he was lost, and is found.' And they began to make merry.

"Now his elder son was in the field; and as he came and drew near to the house, he heard music and dancing. And he called one of the servants and asked what this meant. And he said to him, 'Your brother has come, and your father has killed the fatted calf, because he has received him safe and sound.' But he was angry and refused to go in. His father came out and entreated him, but he answered his father, 'Lo, these many years I have served you, and I never disobeyed your command; yet you never gave me a kid, that I might make merry with my friends. But when this son of yours came, who has devoured your living with harlots, you killed for him the fatted calf!' And he said to him, 'Son, you are always with me, and all that is mine is yours. It was fitting to make merry and be glad, for this your brother was dead, and is alive; he was lost, and is found.'" Luke 15:11-32

Parables

Frame # 4

Read the parables given in the exhibit on the opposite page to determine whether members of a family today might act like the characters pictured in these parables.

By drawing a line through them, cross out the sentences below that make incorrect inferences about the two parables given in the exhibit.

a. In parable A neither son fully did his father's will.

b. Both sons said one thing and then did another. Therefore, parable A is not like family life today, for sons do what they say they will do.

c. In parable B the elder brother thought the father did not love him as much as he loved the spendthrift younger brother.

d. The conduct of the forgiving father is not realistic for no father today would forgive such a son.

e. The conduct of the characters in both parables is understandable in terms of family life today: these parables show genuine insight into family relationships.

f. Relationships within a family move on an altogether different level today. Sons have too much pride to admit their mistakes and fathers do not expect their sons to work for them.

ANSWER to Frame # 4

a. In parable A neither son fully did his father's will.

b. ~~Both sons said one thing and then did another. Therefore, parable A is not like family life today, for sons do what they say they will do.~~

c. In parable B the elder brother thought the father did not love him as much as he loved the spendthrift younger brother.

d. ~~The conduct of the forgiving father is not realistic for no father today would forgive such a son.~~

e. The conduct of the characters in both parables is understandable in terms of family life today: these parables show genuine insight into family relationships.

f. ~~Relationships within a family move on an altogether different level today. Sons have too much pride to admit their mistakes and fathers do not expect their sons to work for them.~~

Parables

Frame # 5

Read the parables given below in order to determine what aspect of life is portrayed in them.

I. "Or what woman, having ten silver coins, if she loses one coin, does not light a lamp and sweep the house and seek diligently until she finds it? And when she has found it, she calls together her friends and neighbors, saying, 'Rejoice with me, for I have found the coin which I had lost.' Even so, I tell you, there is joy before the angels of God over one sinner who repents." Luke 15:8-10

II. "No one sews a piece of unshrunk cloth on an old garment; if he does, the patch tears away from it, the new from the old, and a worse tear is made." Mark 2:21

III. He told them another parable. "The kingdom of heaven is like leaven which a woman took and hid in three measures of meal, till it was all leavened." Matthew 13:33

Place an X before the correct answers in the questions below.

1. The following activities are portrayed in the above parables.

    ___ a. patching clothes   ___ b. making bread

    ___ c. washing clothes   ___ d. sweeping the house

2. The parables picture the daily round of ___ business life.

                                             ___ domestic chores.

ANSWER to Frame # 5

1.
    _X_ a. patching clothes   _X_ b. making bread

    ___ c. washing clothes   _X_ d. sweeping the house

2. The parables picture the daily round of ___ business life.

                                             _X_ domestic chores.

Perhaps as you read the parables in the previous frames you became increasingly aware that people do not think in terms of parables today. Consequently, you need training in the parable as a form of expression in order to develop skills in the interpretation of parables.

Parables

Frame # 6

A Parable is a form of expression that makes a comparison in a certain way. However, since comparisons can be made in different ways, begin your study of parables by noting the different kinds of comparisons given below.

Group A.

    It is hot as an oven outside today.

    Her tears flowed like rain.

Group B

    The desert was a blazing fire today.

    Her tears were a fountain that flowed day and night.

1. Underline the correct words above.

    Terms such as "different from," "similar to," "just as," signal that a comparison is being made. Underline the words that make comparisons in Group A above.

2. Underline the element that makes each statement correct.

    a. In Group B the sentence about the desert (gives the true temperature) (implies that the temperature was as high as it would be in the midst of a blazing fire).

    b. In Group B the sentence about the lady's eyes (*measures* the extent of the tears in that a fountain constantly pours forth a stream of water when the water supply is continuous)(*compares* the extent of her tears with the flow of a fountain).

    c. Thus the sentences in Group B (do not make comparisons)(make comparisons by implying the words "like" or "as").

3. Underline the element that makes each statement correct.

    a. Those comparisons that use the words "like" and "as" can be described as (signalled)(unsignalled).

    b. Those comparisons made without the help of the special words "like" and "as" can be described as (signalled)(unsignalled).

Parables

ANSWER to Frame # 6

1.
Terms such as "different from," "similar to," "just as," <u>signal</u> that a comparison is being made. Underline the words that make comparisons in Group A above.

Group A

It is hot <u>as</u> an oven outside today.

Her tears flowed <u>like</u> rain.

2.
  a. In Group B the sentence about the desert (gives the true temperature) <u>(implies that the temperature was as high as it would be in the midst of a blazing fire)</u>.

  b. In Group B the sentence about the lady's eyes (*measures* the extent of the tears in that a fountain constantly pours forth a stream of water when the water supply is continuous)<u>(*compares* the extent of her tears with the flow of a fountain)</u>.

  c. Thus the sentences in Group B (do not make comparisons)<u>(make comparisons by implying the words "like" or "as")</u>.

3.
  a. Those comparisons that use the words "like" and "as" can be described as (<u>signalled</u>)(unsignalled).

  b. Those comparisons made without the help of the special words "like" and "as" can be described as (signalled)(<u>unsignalled</u>).

Parables

Frame # 7

Separate the statements that contain an *unsignalled* comparison from those that contain a *signalled* comparison by circling the numbers of those statements containing an *unsignalled* comparison.

1. Mercy falls like the gentle dew from heaven.
2. The headlines screamed their anger.
3. Her emotions boiled over.
4. Ours is a cut-flower civilization.
5. She has cheeks like roses.
6. He is strong as an ox.
7. The road is a ribbon winding over the hills.
8. Your kisses are wine.

ANSWER to Frame # 7

2, 3, 4, 7, 8 are statements containing an unsignalled comparison.

Parables

Frame # 8

In the statements below note that the term *subject* is placed over the one element in the unsignalled comparison and the phrase *enlightening parallel* is placed over the other element. Determine which element clarifies or explains the other in a comparison.

	SUBJECT		ENLIGHTENING PARALLEL	
The	desert	was a	blazing fire	today.

	SUBJECT	ENLIGHTENING PARALLEL
Her	emotions	boiled over.

Place a check before the correct statements given below.

1. Describe the relationship between the *subject* and the *enlightening parallel* in the unsignalled comparisons given above.

    ___ a. "Blazing fire" expresses an observer's feelings about the desert and "boiled over" tells how someone felt about another person's emotions: so the *enlightening parallel* clarifies the *subject*.

    ___ b. "Desert" points to a person's reaction to a blazing fire and "emotions" shows the way someone reacted to water boiling over; so the *subject* clarifies the *enlightening parallel*.

2. Which statement characterizes the unsignalled comparisons above?

    ___ a. The dissimilarity [between two things] is pointed out.

    ___ b. A word or phrase, ordinarily applied to one thing [like liquid in a pan on a hot stove] is now used to describe another [like emotions].

Parables

ANSWER to Frame # 8

1.
   ✓ a. "Blazing fire" expresses an observer's feelings about the desert and "boiled over" tells how someone felt about another person's emotions: so the *enlightening parallel* clarifies the *subject*.

   ___ b. "Desert" points to a person's reaction to a blazing fire and "emotions" shows the way someone reacted to water boiling over; so the *subject* clarifies the *enlightening parallel*.

2.
   ___ a. The dissimilarity [between two things] is pointed out.

   ✓ b. A word or phrase, ordinarily applied to one thing [like liquid in a pan on a hot stove] is now used to describe another [like emotions].

Parables

Frame # 9

Read the sentences below and determine whether they are signalled comparisons, unsignalled comparisons, or statements without comparisons.

1. "You are the salt of the earth..." Matthew 5:13a

2. "You are the light of the world." Matthew 5:14a

3. "A city set on a hill cannot be hid." Matthew 5:14b

4. Last night the wind blew down the old apple tree in our back yard.

5. Life is like a bowl of cherries.

6. "If a kingdom is divided against itself, that kingdom cannot stand." Mark 3:24

7. "As he landed he saw a great throng, and he had compassion on them, because they were like sheep without a shepherd..." Mark 6:34

8. "Behold, I send you out as sheep in the midst of wolves; so be wise as serpents and innocent as doves." Matthew 10:16

9. "The eye is the lamp of the body." Matthew 6:22a

Complete the following statements by selecting the numbers of the sentences above and then writing them in the appropriate blanks below. Then write why you classified these sentences as you did.

a. The signalled comparisons are ___, ___, and ___. They should be classified as signalled comparisons because _____

_____

b. The unsignalled comparisons are ___, ___, and ___. They should be classified as unsignalled comparisons because _____

_____

c. The statements without comparisons are ___, ___, and ___. They should not be classified as comparisons because _____

_____

ANSWER to Frame # 9

a. The signalled comarisons are 5 , 7 , and 8 . They should be classified as signalled comparisons because *the comparison is made with the help of special words such as, "like" "as".*

If your answer does not agree substantially with the above answer, go back and study Frame # 6.

b. The unsignalled comparisons are 1 , 2 , and 9 . They should be classified as unsignalled comparisons because *the comparison is made without the help of special words.*

If your answer does not agree substantially with the above answer, go back and study Frame # 6.

c. The statements without comparisons are 3 , 4 , and 6 . They should not be classified as comparisons because *no comparison is involved.*

Parables

Frame # 10

In a previous frame the terms *Subject*, *Enlightening Parallel* were placed over the two elements of an unsignalled comparison. Note that a third term *Relationship* has been added. Determine the use of these terms in the example.

	Subject	Relationship	Enlightening Parallel
Example: The	desert	was	a blazing fire today.
I. The	road	is	a ribbon winding over the hills.
II. Her	eyes	were	fountains that flowed day and night.

1. Match each term below with the sentence describing its use by placing the letter of the sentence on the blank before the term.

   ___ *Subject*   x. This element furnishes the focus of a comparison.

   ___ *Relationship*   y. This element clarifies or explains the focus of a comparison.

   ___ *Enlightening Parallel*   z. This element establishes an *identity* between two things since one thing is spoken of as if it were another.

2. Write *Subject*, *Relationship*, *Enlightening Parallel* over the proper words in I and II above.

ANSWER to Frame # 10

1.
   x *Subject*   x. This element furnishes the focus of a comparison.

   z *Relationship*   y. This element clarifies or explains the focus of a comparison.

   y *Enlightening Parallel*   z. This element establishes an *identity* between two things since one thing is spoken of as if it were another.

2.
	Subject	Relationship	Enlightening Parallel
I. The	road	is	a ribbon winding over the hills.
II. Her	Subject eyes	Relationship were	Enlightening Parallel fountains that flowed day and night.

Exhibit for Frame # 11

The walls of the town were well built; yea, so fast and firm were they knit and compacted together, that had it not been for the townsmen themselves, they could not have been shaken or broken for ever. For here lay the excellent wisdom of him that built Mansoul, that the walls could never be broken down nor hurt by the most mighty adverse potentates, unless, the townsmen gave consent thereto.

This famous town of Mansoul had five gates, at which to come out, and at which to go in; and these were made likewise answerable to the walls, to wit, impregnable, and such as never could be opened nor forced, but by the will and leave of these within. The names of the gates are these: Ear-gate, Eye-gate, Mouth-gate, Nose-gate, and Feel-gate.................................
There was not a rogue, rascal, or traitorous person then within its walls; they were all true men, and fast joined together; and this you know is a great matter. And to all these, it had always, so long as it had the goodness to keep true to Shaddai, the King, his countenance, his protection, and it was his delight that they should remain so for ever.

Well; upon a time there was one Diabolus, a mighty giant, made an assault upon the famous town of Mansoul, to take it, and make it his own habitation. This giant was king of the Black-hearts, and a most raving prince he was. We will, if you please, first discourse of the original of this Diabolus, and then of his taking of this famous town of Mansoul.[1]

[1] John Bunyan, *The Holy War made by King Shaddai upon Diabolus for the Regaining of the Metropolis of the world; or, the losing and taking of the town of Mansoul.* Derby and Jackson, 119 Nassau Street, New York, 1857. p.71.

Parables

Frame # 11

Given in the exhibit on the opposite page is another type of unsignalled comparison called an allegory. Read the allegory and then learn to determine the meaning of the allegory by following the steps outlined below.

1. Begin by performing this simple exercise. A list of enlightening parallels found in the allegory is given below in the left-hand column of this page. Unsignalled "subjects" to which the key phrases refer are given in the right-hand column. Draw a line between an enlightening parallel and its appropriate unsignalled subject. For example, John Bunyan tells us that the different kinds of gates refer to the five senses.

Enlightening Parallels	Unsignalled Subjects
town of Mansoul	God
Ear-gate, Eye-gate, Mouth-gate, Nose-gate, and Feel-gate	the devil
Shaddai, the King	the five senses
Diabolus, a mighty giant	the soul or spiritual life of a man
Black-hearts	the devil's followers

Now reflect on what you did by circling the letter of the answer that makes the following statements true.

2. Inspect the story as a whole and think about the enlightening parallels, such as Mansoul, Black-hearts, Ear-gate, etc. Now ask yourself the question: do these names appear to be

   a. artificial and contrived?   b. natural, like other names of people and places?

3. When the above is the case, the questions to ask in order to discover the unsignalled subjects of an allegory are:

   a. What is the town of Mansoul?   b. What is the *dictionary meaning* of every key phrase?
   and   and
   Who is Shaddai the King?   Is it *good grammar?*

Parables

ANSWER to Frame # 11

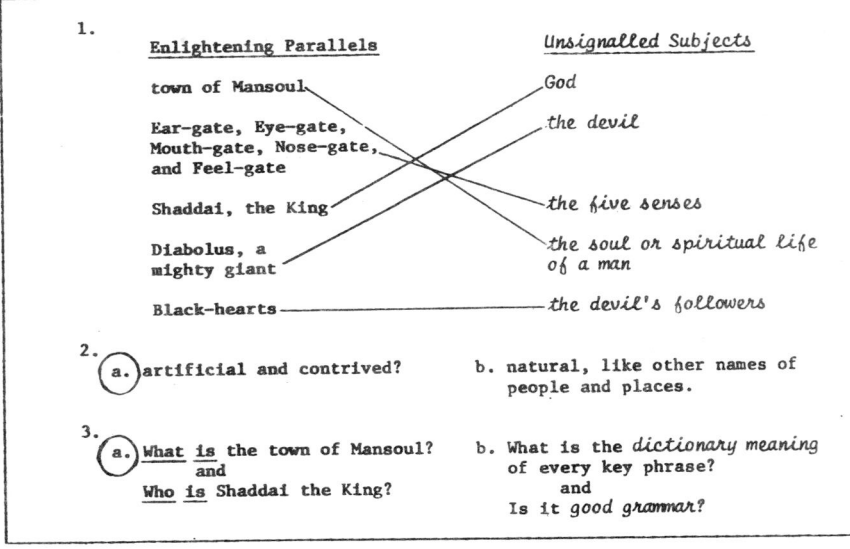

1.
Enlightening Parallels	Unsignalled Subjects
town of Mansoul	God
Ear-gate, Eye-gate, Mouth-gate, Nose-gate, and Feel-gate	the devil
Shaddai, the King	the five senses
Diabolus, a mighty giant	the soul or spiritual life of a man
Black-hearts	the devil's followers

Matches: town of Mansoul — the soul or spiritual life of a man; Ear-gate, Eye-gate, Mouth-gate, Nose-gate, and Feel-gate — the five senses; Shaddai, the King — God; Diabolus, a mighty giant — the devil; Black-hearts — the devil's followers.

2. (a.) artificial and contrived?   b. natural, like other names of people and places.

3. (a.) What *is* the town of Mansoul?   b. What is the *dictionary meaning*
    and   of every key phrase?
    Who *is* Shaddai the King?   and
                                             Is it *good grammar?*

Parables

Exhibit for Frame #12

	SUBJECT	RELATIONSHIP	ENLIGHTENING PARALLEL
I.	The road	is	a ribbon winding over the hills.

II. The walls of the town were well built; yea, so fast and firm were they knit and compacted together, that had it not been for the townsmen themselves, they could not have been shaken or broken for ever. For here lay the excellent wisdom of him that built Mansoul, that the walls could never be broken down nor hurt by the most mighty adverse potentates, unless, the townsmen gave consent thereto.

This famous town of Mansoul had five gates, at which to come out, and at which to go in; and these were made likewise answerable to the walls, to wit, impregnable, and such as never could be opened nor forced, but by the will and leave of these within. The names of the gates are these: Ear-gate, Eye-gate, Mouth-gate, Nose-gate, and Feel-gate................................. There was not a rogue, rascal, or traitorous person then within its walls; they were all true men, and fast joined together; and this you know is a great matter. And to all these, it had always, so long as it had the goodness to keep true to Shaddai, the King, his countenance, his protection, and it was his delight that they should remain so for ever.

Well; upon a time there was one Diabolus, a mighty giant, made an assault upon the famous town of Mansoul, to take it, and make it his own habitation. This giant was king of the Black-hearts, and a most raving prince he was. We will, if you please, first discourse of the origin of this Diabolus, and then of his taking of this famous town of Mansoul.[1]

---

[1] John Bunyan, The Holy War made by King Shaddai upon Diabolus for the Regaining of the Metropolis of the world; or, the losing and taking of the town of Mansoul. Derby and Jackson, 119 Nassau Street, New York, 1857. p. 71.

Parables

Frame #12

Given in the exhibit on the opposite page are an allegory and an unsignalled comparison over which the terms SUBJECT, RELATIONSHIP, ENLIGHTENING PARALLEL are placed. Apply the terms to the allegory in order to show the relationship between the ENLIGHTENING PARALLELS and their unsignalled SUBJECTS.

Underline the responses which make the following statements correct.

1. Apply the (above) terms to the allegory.

   a. The unsignalled subjects of the allegory deal with (the capture of a town by a mighty giant) (a man's spiritual life).

   b. An enlightening parallel of the allegory is (town of Mansoul) (a man's spiritual life).

   c. Since the allegory is saying that Ear-gate is the sense of hearing, the RELATIONSHIP in the allegory is one of (identity since one thing is spoken of as if it were another) (similarly since the work "like" is used in making the comparison).

   d. The allegory may omit elements, as you can see in the exhibit. The elements(s) omitted is/are: (SUBJECT) (RELATIONSHIP) (ENLIGHTENING PARALLEL).

2. What is the relationship between the ENLIGHTENING PARALLEL and its unsignalled SUBJECT in the allegory?

   a. In the unsignalled comparison on the opposite page ("the road" clarifies or is a way of describing "a ribbon winding over the hills") ("a ribbon winding over the hills" clarifies or is a way of describing "the road").

   b. In the allegory ("town of Mansoul" enlightens, or is a way of describing, "the spiritual life of a man") ("the spiritual life of a man" enlightens, or is a way of describing, "town of Mansoul").

Parables

ANSWER to Frame #12

1.
- a. The unsignalled subjects of the allegory deal with (the capture of town by a mighty giant) (<u>a man's spiritual life</u>).

- b. An enlightening parallel of the allegory is (<u>town of Mansoul</u>) (a man's spiritual life).

- c. Since the allegory is saying that Ear-gate is the sense of hearing, the RELATIONSHIP in the allegory is one of (<u>identity since one thing is spoken of as if it were</u> another) (similarity since the word "like" is used in making the comparison).

- d. The allegory may omit elements, as you can see in the exhibit. The element(s) omitted is/are: (<u>SUBJECT</u>) (<u>RELATIONSHIP</u>) (ENLIGHTENING PARALLEL).

2.
- a. In the unsignalled comparison on the opposite page ("the road" clarifies or is a way of describing "a ribbon winding over the hills") ("<u>a ribbon winding over the hills" clarifies</u> or is a <u>way of describing</u> "the road").

- b. In the allegory ("<u>town of Mansoul" enlightens, or is a way of describing</u>, "<u>the spiritual life of a man</u>") ("the spiritual life of a man" enlightens, or is a way of describing, "town of Mansoul").

Parables

Exhibit for Frame #13

A. "The kingdom of heaven may be compared to a king who gave a marriage feast for his son, and sent his servants to call those who were invited to the marriage feast; but they would not come. Again he sent other servants, saying, 'Tell those who are invited, Behold, I have made ready my dinner, my oxen and my fat calves are killed, and everything is ready; come to the marriage feast.' But they made light of it and went off, one to his farm, another to his business, while the rest seized his servants, treated them shamefully, and killed them. The king was angry, and he sent his troops and destroyed those murderers and burned their city. Then he said to his servants, 'The wedding is ready, but those invited were not worthy. Go therefore to the thoroughfares, and invite to the marriage feast as many as you find.' And those servants went out into the streets and gathered all whom they found, both bad and good; so the wedding hall was filled with guests."
Matthew 22:2-10

B. But he said to him, "A man once gave a great banquet, and invited many; and at the time for the banquet he sent his servant to say to those who had been invited, 'Come; for all is now ready.' But they all alike began to make excuses. The first said to him, 'I have bought a field, and I must go out and see it; I pray you, have me excused.' And another said, 'I have bought five yoke of oxen, and I go to examine them; I pray you, have me excused.' And another said, 'I have married a wife, and therefore I cannot come.' So the servant came and reported this to his master. Then the householder in anger said to his servant, 'Go out quickly to the streets and lanes of the city, and bring in the poor and maimed and blind and lame.' And the servant said, "Sir, what you commanded has been done, and still there is room.' And the master said to the servant, 'Go out to the highways and hedges, and compel people to come in, that my house may be filled. For I tell you, none of those men who were invited shall taste my banquet.'"
Luke 14:16-24

Parables

Frame #13

Read both stories given in the exhibit on the opposite page to determine which contains artificial or contrived elements. Then test your skill in labeling the parts of the allegory.

Answer the following questions by placing the letter of the correct element on the appropriate blanks.

1. Given below are a list of elements taken from the allegory on the opposite page. Those elements that appear to be artificial or contrived are ____ and ____.

   a. a king gave a wedding feast for his son

   b. the king sent servants to call the guests when the feast was ready

   c. the guests beat up and killed the king's servants

   d. the king invited other guests to replace those who did not come

   e. the king destroyed the guests who refused to come and burned their city

2. Given below are a list of sentences, each of which contains a blank. The sentences review what you have learned in previous frames about the terms designating the parts of an allegory. Beneath the sentences are a list of possible answers each of which is preceded by a letter. Complete the following sentences by placing the letter of the correct word or phrase on the appropriate blank.

   The elements (see question #1 above) that appear in print in the allegory have been named the ____.

   The elements that appear in print in the allegory enlighten or are a way of describing the ____.

   The relationship between the enlightening parallel and the unsignalled subject of an allegory is one of ____ since one element is spoken of as if it were another.

   The crucial questions to ask in order to determine the meaning of an allegory are ____.

   a. unsignalled subjects   b. enlightening parallels

   c. <u>What is</u>? and <u>Who is</u>?   d. similarity

   e. identity   f. unsignalled comparison

Parables

ANSWER to Frame #13

1.
Those elements that appear to be artificial or contrived are __c__ and __e__.

   a. a king gave a wedding feast for his son

   b. the king sent servants to call the guests when the feast was ready

   c. the guests beat up and killed the king's servants

   d. the king destroyed the guests who refused to come and burned their city

2.
The elements (see question #1 above) that appear in print in the allegory have been named the __b__.

The elements that appear in print in the allegory enlighten or are a way of describing the __a__.

The relationship between the enlightening parallel and the unsignalled subject of an allegory is one of __e__ since one element is spoken of as if it were another.

The crucial questions to ask in order to determine the meaning of an allegory are __c__.

   a. unsignalled subjects   b. enlightening parallels

   c. <u>What is?</u> and <u>Who is?</u>   d. similarity

   e. identity   f. unsignalled comparison

Parables

Frame #14

Given below is the same allegory used in Frame #13. Explore the details of the allegory in order to determine its meaning.

"The kingdom of heaven may be compared to a king who gave a marriage feast for his son, and sent his servants to call those who were invited to the marriage feast; but they would not come. Again he sent other servants, saying, 'Tell those who are invited, Behold, I have made ready my dinner, my oxen and my fat calves are killed, and everything is ready; come to the marriage feast.' But they made light of it and went off, one to his farm, another to his business, while the rest seized his servants, treated them shamefully, and killed them. The king was angry, and he sent his troops and destroyed those murderers and burned their city. Then he said to his servants, 'The wedding is ready, but those invited were not worthy. Go therefore to the thoroughfares, and invite to the marriage feast as many as you find.' And those servants went out into the streets and gathered all whom they found, both bad and good; so the wedding hall was filled with guests."

1. A list of Enlightening Parallels found in the allegory is given below in the left-hand column. Unsignalled Subjects to which the Enlightening Parallels refer are given in the right-hand column. Match them up by placing the letter of the Unsignalled Subjects on the blank before the appropriate Enlightening Parallels.

   Enlightening Parallels   Unsignalled Subjects

   ____ 1. a king   a. the feast of salvation

   ____ 2. the marriage feast   b. Christian evangelists to Israel

   ____ 3. his son   c. God

   ____ 4. first group of servants d. Jesus

   ____ 5. second group of servants e. Old Testament prophets

   ____ 6. burning the city   f. fall of Jerusalem to Rome AD 70

   ____ 7. inviting "as many as you g. mission of the church to those
           find"   outside official Judaism

2. Again match up the appropriate Unsignalled Subject with the Enlightening Parallel found in the left-hand column.

   ____ 1. The king invited others a. God offered salvation to others
           when the guests repeatedly   when Israel repeatedly rejected
           refused to come.   his invitation.

                                    b. It is safer to go to a wedding
                                       than to beat up the person who
                                       brings the invitation.

Parables

ANSWER to Frame #14

1.
Enlightening Parallels	Unsignalled Subjects
_c_ 1. a king	a. *the feast of salvation*
_a_ 2. the marriage feast	b. *Christian evangelists to Israel*
_d_ 3. his son	c. *God*
_e_ 4. first group of servants	d. *Jesus*
_b_ 5. second group of servants	e. *Old Testament prophets*
_f_ 6. burning the city	f. *fall of Jerusalem to Rome AD 70*
_g_ 7. inviting "as many as you find"	g. *mission of the church to those outside official Judaism*

2.
    _a_ 1. The king invited others when the guests repeatedly refused to come.

    a. *God offered salvation to others when Israel repeatedly rejected his invitation.*

    b. *It is safer to go to a wedding than to beat up the person who brings the invitation.*

Parables

Frame #15

Given below is the same allegory from the New Testament that you analysed in the previous frame. Do the <u>formal</u> characteristics of the allegory from the New Testament resemble those of the allegory Mansoul?

"The kingdom of heaven may be compared to a king who gave a marriage feast for his son, and sent his servants to call those who were invited to the marriage feast; but they would not come. Again he sent other servants, saying, 'Tell those who are invited, Behold, I have made ready my dinner, my oxen and my fat calves are killed, and everything is ready; come to the marriage feast.' But they made light of it and went off, one to his farm, another to his business, while the rest seized his servants, treated them shamefully, and killed them. The king was angry, and he sent his troops and destroyed those murderers and burned their city. Then he said to his servants, 'The wedding is ready, but those invited were not worthy. Go therefore to the thoroughfares, and invite to the marriage feast as many as you find.' And those servants went out into the streets and gathered all whom they found, both bad and good; so the wedding hall was filled with guests."

1. Place a check before those characteristics that describe the allegory from the New Testament.

    ____ a. The allegory contains a series of unsignalled subjects.

    ____ b. The unsignalled subjects are inferred from the allegory by asking the questions: Who is (the king): What is (the city)? etc.

    ____ c. The enlightening parallels, like "king" and "burned their city" are less artificial than those in the allegory Mansoul.

    ____ d. The relationship between the unsginalled subject and the enlightening parallel is best expressed by the verb "is" since one thing is spoken of as if it were another.

2. Check the answer that accurately describes the New TEstament allegory.

The formal characteristics of the New Testament allegory

    ____ a. are different from those of other allegories.
    ____ b. resemble those of other allegories.

ANSWER to Frame #15

1. a, b, c, d, all describe the New Testament allegory.   2. b.

WE NOW TURN TO PARABLES - a very different form from the allegory.

Parables

Frame #16

Now look at a parable (example III below), one kind of signalled comparison. Discover how the signalled comparisons, given below in example II and III, differ from an unsignalled comparison.

       subject   *relationship*   *enlightening parallel*
I. Her tears   were   fountains that flowed day and night.

II. Her tears   were like   fountains that flowed day and night.

III. What is the kingdom of God like?   And to what shall I compare it?

It   is like   a grain of mustard seed which a man took and sowed in his garden; and it grew and became a tree, and the birds of the air made nests in its branches.   Luke 13:18-19

1. Given below are two columns, designating signalled comparisons and unsignalled comparisons, and a list of characterics that apply to various kinds of comparisons. The characteristics may apply to one, both or neither column. Place an X under the appropriate column which a given characteristic describes.

Signalled   Unsignalled
Comparisons Comparisons

   ____   ____   1. The subject is given in print.

   ____   ____   2. The unsignalled subject must be inferred from the enlightening parallel.

   ____   ____   3. The relationship between the subject and the enlightening parallel is one of identity since one thing is spoken of as if it were another.

   ____   ____   4. The relationship between the subject and the enlightening parallel is one of similarity since a word, such as "like", is used in making the comparison.

2. Write the words, *subject, relationship, enlightening parallel* over the appropriate parts of II and III.

Parables

ANSWER to Frame #16

1.
Signalled Comparisons	Unsignalled Comparisons		
X	X	1.	The subject is given in print.
___	___	2.	The unsignalled subject must be inferred from the enlightening parallel.
___	X	3.	The relationship between the subject and the enlightening parallel is one of <u>identity</u> since one thing is spoken of as if it were another.
X	___	4.	The relationship between the subject and the enlightening parallel is one of <u>similarity</u> since a word, such as "like", is used in making the comparison.

2.
   II. <u>*subject*</u> <u>*relationship*</u> <u>   *enlightening parallel*   </u>
       Her tears were like fountains that flowed day and night.

                 subject
  III. What is the <u>kingdom of God</u> like? And to what shall I compare it?

      relationship
    It <u>is like</u> a grain of mustard seed which a man took and

<u>   *enlightening parallel*   </u>
sowed in his garden; and it grew and became a tree, and the birds

<u>of the air made nests in its branches.</u>   Luke 13:18-19

Parables

Exhibit for Frame # 17

Parable	Commentary
And again he said, "To what shall I compare the [Subject] kingdom of God?	The Kingdom of God is the proper relationship between God and men which emphasizes God's kingly rule in human life. Thus Jesus said, "Thy kingdom come. Thy will be done, on earth as it is in heaven."
It [Relationship] is like [leaven	Leaven (yeast), a small piece of fermenting dough, spreads through the unfermented dough and causes it to rise.
Enlightening Parallel which a woman took and hid	Since there were no bakeries, every housewife baked enough bread each morning for the needs of the day. Bread was more important in the diet of a first century Jew than it is in our diet.
in three measures of meal,	Three measures is more than our bushel. The housewife mixed a small bit of yeast with the dough, covered it, and let "rise" overnight.
] till it was all leavened." Luke 13:20-21	The next morning the yeast had penetrated all the dough. In this parable Jesus is apparently comparing the contrast between the tiny bit of leaven and the great mass of dough it penetrates with the contrast between the tiny beginning of the kingdom and the kingdom's fulfillment.

Parables

Frame # 17

Read the Commentary given in the exhibit on the opposite page in order to interpret the parable. Then, note the importance of the *Relationship* between the *Subject* and the *Enlightening Parallel* in arriving at a correct interpretation.

Circle the statement which correctly describes the proper *Relationship* between the *Subject* and the *Enlightening Parallel* in the parable given in the exhibit.

1. The parable is saying that the Kingdom of God is (is being identified with) leaven hidden in three measures of meal.

2. The parable is saying that the Kingdom of God is like (is being compared with) leaven hidden in three measures of meal.

ANSWER to Frame # 17

1. The parable is saying that the Kingdom of God is (is being identified with) leaven hidden in three measures of meal.

2. (The parable is saying that the Kingdom of God is like (is being compared with) leaven hidden in three measures of meal)

Parables

Exhibit for Frame # 18

A. A Fable from Judges 9:7-15

When it was told to Jotham, he went and stood on the top of Mount Gerizim, and cried aloud and said to them, "Listen to me, you men of Shechem, that God may listen to you. The trees once went forth to anoint a king over them; and they said to the olive tree, 'Reign over us.' But the olive tree said to them, 'Shall I leave my fatness, by which gods and men are honored, and go to sway over the trees?' And the trees said to the fig tree, 'Come you, and reign over us.' But the fig tree said to them, 'Shall I leave my sweetness and my good fruit, and go to sway over the trees?' And the trees said to the vine, 'Come you, and reign over us.' But the vine said to them, 'Shall I leave my wine which cheers gods and men, and go to sway over the trees?' Then all the trees said to the bramble, 'Come you, and reign over us.' And the bramble said to the trees, 'If in good faith you are anointing me king over you, then come and take refuge in my shade; but if not, let fire come out of the bramble and devour the cedars of Lebanon.'

Interpretation:
You need to know that the olive tree is a very valuable tree, while the bramble is worthless and cannot provide shade for trees. The bramble stands for (is) Abimelech, a wicked man, whom the men of Shechem made their king after the honorable Gideon refused to become king.

B. A Parable from Luke 11:5-8

And he said to them, "Which of you who has a friend will go to him at midnight and say to him, 'Friend, lend me three loaves; for a friend of mine has arrived on a journey, and I have nothing to set before him;' and he will answer from within, 'Do not bother me; the door is now shut, and my children are with me in bed; I cannot get up and give you anything?' I tell you, though he will not get up and give him anything because he is his friend, yet because of his importunity he will rise and give him whatever he needs."

Interpretation:
While the principle of interpretation for this parable will be given in detail later, let it suffice to say this parable is an example of arguing from the lesser to the greater. If the friend within answers the request of his embarrassed neighbor, perhaps only to get rid of the inconvenience, how much more willingly does God answer the requests of his children.

Parables

Frame # 18

Read the stories, along with their respective interpretations, in the exhibit on the opposite page. If you now understand the importance of the relationship of similarity in interpreting a parable, note what happens when you <u>violate</u> that relationship in interpreting a given parable.

1. Treat the parable as an allegory by drawing a line between an enlightening parallel and its appropriate unsignalled subject.

   <u>Enlightening Parallels</u>

   1. three loaves
   2. the friend within
   3. the neighbor
   4. the door is shut
   5. my children...in bed
   6. repeated banging (importunity)
   7. rising and giving the loaves

   <u>Unsignalled Subjects</u>

   a. *God*
   b. *God is not answering prayer*
   c. *God has his own concerns*
   d. *you or me*
   e. *the content of the prayer*
   f. *God ignores his own concerns to fulfill our needs*
   g. *repeated prayer*

2. Compare the meaning of the parable (see exhibit) with the meaning (above) of the allegorized treatment of the parable. Then draw a line between the introductory part of the sentence given below and its appropriate conclusion.

   If you violate the relationship of similarity in interpreting a parable and treat it as an allegory, you

   a. destroy the meaning of the parable.

   b. arrive at the same meaning as if you had taken the relationship of similarity seriously.

Parables

ANSWER to Frame # 18

1.
Enlightening Parallels — Unsignalled Subjects

1. three loaves
2. the friend within
3. the neighbor
4. the door is shut
5. my children...in bed
6. repeated banging (importunity)
7. rising and giving the loaves

a. God
b. God is not answering prayer
c. God has his own concerns
d. you or me
e. the content of the prayer
f. God ignores his own concerns to fulfill our needs
g. repeated prayer

Matches:
1 → e
2 → d
3 → a
4 → b
5 → c
6 → g
7 → f

2.
If you violate the relationship of similarity in interpreting a parable and treat it as an allegory, you ——

a. destroy the meaning of the parable.
b. arrive at the same meaning as if you had taken the relationship of similarity seriously.

Parables

Exhibit for Frame # 19

Parable	Commentary
And he said, "With what can we compare the kingdom of God, [SUBJECT]	The kingdom of God is the proper relationship btween God and men which emphasizes God's kingly rule in human life. Thus Jesus said, "Thy kingdom come. Thy will be done, on earth as it is in heaven."
or what parable shall we use for it? [RELATIONSHIP] It is like [a grain of mustard seed, which, when	The mustard plant was very common in Jesus' day.
ENLIGHTENING PARALLEL sown upon the ground, is the smallest of all the seeds on earth; yet when it is sown it grows up and becomes the greatest of all shrubs, and puts forth large branches, so that the birds of the air can make nests _____] in its shade." Mark 4:30-32	This is another contrast parable in which Jesus is apparently comparing the contrast between the tiny seed and the great shrub with the contrast between the tiny beginning of the kingdom in his ministry and the kingdom's fulfillment.

Parables

Frame # 19

Study the parable along with its accompanying commentary to discover the nature of the enlightening parallel and the kind of subject matter dealt with in the parable.

Underline the phrase that correctly completes the following statements.

1. Judging by the parable on the opposite page, the <u>enlightening parallel</u> of the parable is (a topic drawn from the everyday experience of the people of that time) (a specifically religious kind of topic).

2. Judging by the parable on the opposite page, the <u>subject</u> deals with (some aspect of God's relationship to men) (the agricultural practices of the time).

3. Thus, the kingdom of God is clarified or explained by a (kind of story that only religious people would know) (kind of story that everyone would know).

4. The enlightening parallel of a parable is (artificial and contrived) (natural and uncontrived).

ANSWER to Frame # 19

1. Judging by the parable on the opposite page, the <u>enlightening parallel</u> of the parable is (<u>a topic drawn from the everyday experience of the people of that time</u>) (a specifically religious kind of topic).

2. Judging by the parable on the opposite page, the <u>subject</u> deals with (<u>some aspect of God's relationahip to men</u>) (the agricultural practices of the time).

3. Thus, the kingdom of God is clarified or explained by a (kind of story that only religious people would know) (<u>kind of story that everyone would know</u>).

4. The enlightening parallel of a parable is (artificial and contrived) (<u>natural and uncontrived</u>).

Parables

Frame # 20

Sometimes we learn more about a parable by comparing it with what it is not than by directly seeking what it is. Given below are a fable from Aesop and a parable. Note that the parable treats the enlightening parallel in a specific way.

    A crow having stolen a bit of flesh, perched in a tree, and held it in her beak. A fox seeing her, longed to possess himself of the flesh; and by a wily stratagem succeeded. "How handsome is the crow," he exclaimed, "in the beauty of her shape and in the fairness of her complexion! O, if her voice were only equal to her beauty, she would deservedly be considered the Queen of Birds!" This he said deceitfully; but the crow, anxious to refute the reflection cast upon her voice, set up a loud caw, and dropped the flesh. The fox quickly picked it up, and thus addressed the crow: "My good crow, your voice is right enough, but your wit is wanting."

    So he told them this parable: "What man of you, having a hundred sheep, if he has lost one of them, does not leave the ninety-nine in the wilderness, and go after the one which is lost, until he finds it? And when he has found it, he lays it on his shoulders, rejoicing. And when he comes home, he calls together his friends and his neighbors, saying to them, 'Rejoice with me, for I have found my sheep which was lost.' Just so, I tell you, there will be more joy in heaven over one sinner who repents..." Luke 15:3-7

Compare the enlightening parallel in the parable with the enlightening parallel in the fable by *circling* "P" when a correct statement is made about the parable and "F" when a correct statement is made about the fable.

    P   F   The animals of the field are given speech.

    P   F   If animals or plants are mentioned in the story, they do not speak.

    P   F   If people in the story speak, they are true-to-life and their speech is true to their function or character.

    P   F   The story teaches a maxim such as: flatterers are not to be trusted.

    P   F   The story of itself does not teach anything.

    P   F   The story exhibits an artificial quality.

    P   F   The story exhibits an everyday, uncontrived quality.

ANSWER to Frame # 20

P	(F)	The animals of the field are given speech.
(P)	F	If animals or plants are mentioned in the story, they do not speak.
(P)	F	If people in the story speak, they are true-to-life and their speech is true to their function or character.
P	(F)	The story teaches a maxim such as: flatterers are not to be trusted.
(P)	F	The story of itself does not teach anything.
P	(F)	The story exhibits an artificial quality.
(P)	F	The story exhibits an everyday, uncontrived quality.

Parables

Exhibit for Frame # 21

Parable	Commentary
"For the kingdom of heaven is like a householder who went out early in the morning to hire laborers for his vineyard. After agreeing with the laborers for a denarius a day, he sent them into his vineyard. And going out about the third hour he saw others standing idle in the marketplace; and to them he said, 'You go into the vineyard too, and whatever is right I will give you.' So they went. Going out again about the sixth hour and the ninth hour, he did the same. And about the eleventh hour he went out and found others standing; and he said to them, 'Why do you stand here idle all day?' They said to him, 'Because no one has hired us.' He said to them, 'You go into the vineyard too.' And when evening came, the owner of the vineyard said to his steward, 'Call the laborers and pay them their wages, beginning with the last, up to the first.' And when those hired about the eleventh hour came, each of them received a denarius. Now when the first came, they thought they would receive more; but each of them also received a denarius. And on receiving it they grumbled at the householder, saying, 'These last worked only one hour, and you have made them equal to us who have borne the burden of the day and the scorching heat.' But he replied to one of them, 'Friend, I am doing you no wrong; did you not agree with me for a denarius? Take what belongs to you, and go; I choose to give to this last as I give to you. Am I not allowed to do what I choose with what belongs to me? Or do you begrudge my generosity?'" Matthew 20:1-15	In Jesus' day many small farms had been consolidated into large holdings which hired and paid laborers on a daily basis. A denarius was a day's wage. It was sufficient for life, but not generous by our standards. Since there were no clocks, the hours of the day were counted from the rising of the sun. Hence "third hour" means about 8:30 A.M. Grapes had to be picked and pressed before the rainy season. Perhaps this explains why he kept hiring.

Frame # 21

Examine the parable and accompanying commentary in the exhibit on the opposite page to determine whether it illustrates the "everydayness" of the parables of Jesus.

1. Place a check before the statements that accurately describe the parable on the opposite page.

　　___ a. As the attitude of the workers shows, it was the usual practice to pay the same wage to all laborers, regardless of whether they had worked one hour or the whole day.

　　___ b. As the grumbling of the workmen shows, the action of the householder did not make good sense.

　　___ c. The story contains an unusual feature or unexpected happening.

　　___ d. A surprising development makes nonsense of the whole story.

　　___ e. A surprising development in a parable accents the everydayness of the story because surprising things sometimes happen in the midst of everyday life.

ANSWER to Frame # 21

1.
　　___ a. As the attitude of the workers shows, it was the usual practice to pay the same wage to all laborers, regardless of whether they had worked one hour or the whole day.

　　✓ b. As the grumbling of the workmen shows, the action of the householder did not make good sense.

　　✓ c. The story contains an unusual feature or unexpected happening.

　　___ d. A surprising development makes nonsense of the whole story.

　　✓ e. A surprising development in a parable accents the everydayness of the story because surprising things sometimes happen in the midst of everyday life.

Parables

Exhibit for Frame # 22

And he said, "There was a man who had two sons; and the younger of them said to his father, 'Father, give me the share of property that falls to me.' And he divided his living between them. Not many days later, the younger son gathered all he had and took his journey into a far country, and there he squandered his property in loose living. And when he had spent everything, a great famine arose in that country, and he began to be in want. So he went and joined himself to one of the citizens of that country, who sent him into his fields to feed swine. And he would gladly have fed on the pods that the swine ate; and no one gave him anything. But when he came to himself he said, 'How many of my father's hired servants have bread enough and to spare, but I perish here with hunger! I will arise and go to my father, and I will say to him, "Father, I have sinned against heaven and before you; I am no longer worthy to be called your son; treat me as one of your hired servants."' And he arose and came to his father. But while he was yet at a distance, his father saw him and had compassion, and ran and embraced him and kissed him. And the son said to him, 'Father, I have sinned against heaven and before you; I am no longer worthy to be called your son.' But the father said to his servants, 'Bring quickly the best robe, and put it on him; and put a ring on his hand, and shoes on his feet; and bring the fatted calf and kill it, and let us eat and make merry; for this my son was dead, and is alive again; he was lost, and is found.' And they began to make merry. Now his elder son was in the field; and as he came and drew near to the house, he heard music and dancing. And he called one of the servants and asked what this meant. And he said to him, 'Your brother has come, and your father has killed the fatted calf, because he has received him safe and sound.' But he was angry and refused to go in. His father came out and entreated him, but he answered his father, 'Lo, these many years I have served you, and I never disobeyed your command; yet you never gave me a kid, that I might make merry with my friends. But when this son of yours came, who has devoured your living with harlots, you killed for him the fatted calf!' And he said to him, 'Son, you are always with me, and all that is mine is yours. It was fitting to make merry and be glad, for this your brother was dead, and is alive; he was lost, and is found.'" Luke 15:11-32

Note: Running was considered highly unusual for an elderly and dignified old man in this culture.
The full forgiveness and reinstatement of the son are shown by the three orders of the father - the giving of the robe, the giving of the ring and shoes, and the killing of the calf.

Note: Sometimes the change in social customs makes us unaware of the impact of a story on its first hearers. The following passage describes the almost absolute power over the family that a father had in Biblical times.

"If a man has a stubborn and rebellious son, who will not obey the voice of his father or the voice of his mother, and, though they chastise him, will not give heed to them, then his father and his mother shall take hold of him and bring him out to the elders of his city at the gate of the place where he lives, and they shall say to the elders of his city, 'This our son is stubborn and rebellious, he will not obey our voice, he is a glutton and a drunkard.' Then all the men of the city shall stone him to death with stones;..."
Deuteronomy 21:18-21a

Parables

Frame # 22

Read the parable given in the exhibit on the opposite page, along with the notes and legal passage from the Old Testament. Notice that, while the enlightening parallel of a parable is uncontrived, it may be far from ordinary.

Separate the ordinary features of the enlightening parallel from the unusual or unexpected happenings (in the list below) by drawing a line through the ordinary features.

1. A younger son leaves home to make his way in the world.

2. A younger son asks for his share of the father's property before his father's death.

3. The father gives the younger son what he asks.

4. The forgiveness of the father is unrestricted.

5. The older brother is jealous of the favor his father showed to his wastrel younger brother.

ANSWER to Frame # 22

1. ~~A younger son leaves home to make his way in the world.~~

2. A younger son asks for his share of the father's property before his father's death.

3. The father gives the younger son what he asks.

4. The forgiveness of the father is unrestricted.

5. ~~The older brother is jealous of the favor his father showed to his wastrel younger brother.~~

Note: For a complete discussion of the social customs reflected in this parable see Joachim Jeremias, *The Parables of Jesus*, trans. by S. H. Hooke, SCM Press LTD., 1955, pp. 103-106.

Exhibit for Frame # 23

A. But he said to him, "A man once gave a great banquet, and invited many; and at the time for the banquet he sent his servant to say to those who had been invited, 'Come; for all is now ready.' But they all alike began to make excuses. The first said to him, 'I have bought a field, and I must go out and see it; I pray you, have me excused.' And another said, 'I have bought five yoke of oxen, and I go to examine them; I pray you, have me excused.' And another said, 'I have married a wife, and therefore I cannot come.' So the servant came and reported this to his master. Then the householder in anger said to his servant. 'Go out quickly to the streets and lanes of the city, and bring in the poor and maimed and blind and lame.' And the servant said, 'Sir, what you commanded has been done, and still there is room.' And the master said to the servant, 'Go out to the highways and hedges, and compel people to come in, that my house may be filled. For I tell you, none of those men who were invited shall taste my banquet.'" Luke 14:16-24

Then he [the king] said to his servants, 'The wedding is ready, but those invited were not worthy. Go therefore to the thoroughfares, and invite to the marriage feast as many as you find.' And those servants went out into the streets and gathered all whom they found, both bad and good; so the wedding hall was filled with guests.

B. "But when the king came in to look at the guests, he saw there a man who had no wedding garment; and he said to him, 'Friend, how did you get in here without a wedding garment?' And he was speechless. Then the king said to the attendants, 'Bind him hand and foot, and cast him into the outer darkness; there men will weep and gnash their teeth.'" Matthew 22:8-13

Parables

Frame # 23

Read the allegory and the parable given in the exhibit on the opposite page. Then distinguish between the contrived features of the allegory and the uncontrived, but out-of-the-ordinary features of the parable in preparation for determining the distinctive elements of the form parable.

Place the letter of the correct answer on the appropriate blanks in the following sentences.

In order to complete sentences 1 and 2 (below) select from elements a. through d. which have been taken from the stories in the exhibit.

1. The contrived elements in the allegory are ___ and ___.

2. The uncontrived, but out-of-the-ordinary elements in the parable are ___ and ___.

   a. All the invited guests refused to attend the banquet.

   b. The householder then invites anyone whom his servant finds.

   c. Although the king's servants had just invited him in from the thoroughfares, the guest who wore no wedding garment was bound hand and foot and cast into outer darkness.

   d. Outer darkness was a place where men wept and gnashed their teeth.

Describe the *relationship* between the *subjects* and the *enlightening parallels* in the two stories in the exhibit.

3. If the relationship is that of identity in story B, the king ___ God.

4. If the relationship is that of similarity in story A, God ___ a man who, when his invited guests spurn his invitation to dinner, extends his invitation to others.

   e. is   f. is like

Now select the distinctive elements of the form parable.

5. The distinctive elements of the form parable are ___ and ___.

   g. a contrived enlightening parallel   h. a relationship of identity

   i. an uncontrived but, sometimes   j. a relationship of similarity
      out-of-the-ordinary
      enlightening parallel

Parables

ANSWER to Frame # 23

1. The contrived elements in the allegory are _c_ and _d_.
2. The uncontrived, but out-of-the-ordinary elements in the parable are _a_ and _b_.

   a. All the invited guests refused to attend the banquet.

   b. The householder then invites anyone whom his servant finds.

   c. Although the king's servants had just invited him in from the thoroughfares, the guest who wore no wedding garment was bound hand and foot and cast into outer darkness.

   d. Outer darkness was a place where men wept and gnashed their teeth.

   Note: *In the allegory the inspection of the guests by the king is the last judgment and outer darkness is hell.*

3. If the relationship is that of **identity** in story B, the king _e_ God.

4. If the relationship is that of **similarity** in story A, God _f_ a man who, when his invited guests spurn his invitation to dinner, extends his invitation to others.

   e. is   f. is like

5. The distinctive elements of the form parable are _i_ and _j_.

   g. a contrived enlightening parallel   h. a relationship of identity

   i. an uncontrived but, sometimes out-of-the-ordinary enlightening parallel   j. a relationship of similarity

   Note: *If you missed "i" in the above question review Frames 21 and 22. If you missed "j" in the above question review Frames 16 and 17.*

Parables

Frame # 24

Three parables are given below. Write the words *Subject, Relationship,* and *Enlightening Parallel* over the appropriate parts of the parable.

1. And again he said, "To what shall I compare the [____kingdom of God?____]
   It [__is like__] [__leaven which a woman took and hid in three measures of meal, till it was all leavened.__]" Luke 13:20-21

2. And he said, "With what can we compare the [__kingdom of God,__] or what parable shall we use for it? It [__is like__] [__a grain of mustard seed, which, when sown upon the ground, is the smallest of all the seeds on earth; yet when it is sown it grows up and becomes the greatest of all shrubs, and puts forth large branches, so that the birds of the air can make nests in its shade.__]" Mark 4:30-32

3. And he said, "The [__kingdom of God__] [__is as if__] [__a man should scatter seed upon the ground, and should sleep and rise night and day, and the seed should sprout and grow, he knows not how. The earth produces of itself, first the blade, then the ear, then the full grain in the ear. But when the grain is ripe, at once he puts in the sickle, because the harvest has come.__]" Mark 4:26-29

Parables

ANSWER to Frame # 24

1. And again he said, "To what shall I compare the [Subject] kingdom of God?

   [Relationship] [Enlightening Parallel
   It   is like   leaven which a woman took and hid in three

   ]
   measures of meal, till it was all leavened."   Luke 13:20-21

2. And he said, "With what can we compare the [Subject] kingdom of God, or what

   [Relationship] [
   parable shall we use for it? It   is like   a grain of mustard

   seed, which, when sown upon the ground, is the smallest of all the

   Enlightening Parallel
   seeds on earth; yet when it is sown it grows up and becomes the greatest

   of all shrubs, and puts forth large branches, so that the birds of the

   ]
   air can make nests in its shade."   Mark 4:30-32

3. And he said, "The [Subject] [Relationship] [
                     kingdom of God   is as if   a man

   should scatter seed upon the ground, and should sleep and rise night

   and day, and the seed should sprout and grow, he knows not how. The

   Enlightening Parallel
   earth produces of itself, first the blade, then the ear, then the full

   grain in the ear. But when the grain is ripe, at once he puts in the

   ]
   sickle, because the harvest has come."   Mark 4:26-29

Parables

Exhibit for Frame # 25

1. Jesus said: The [kingdom] [is like] [a shepherd] who had a hundred sheep. One of them, the largest, lost his way. He left the ninety-nine and sought the one until he found it. After he had toiled, he said to the sheep, I love you more than the ninety-nine.]¹

   Note: *This version of the Biblical parable is found in a gospel accepted by an heretical group of Christians.*

2. "[Or what woman, having ten silver coins, if she loses one coin, does not light a lamp and sweep the house and seek diligently until she finds it? And when she has found it, she calls together her friends and neighbors,] saying, 'Rejoice with me, for I have found the coin which I had lost.' [Even so,] I tell you, [there is joy before the angels of God over one sinner who repents.]" Luke 15:8-10

¹Robert M. Grant and David N. Freedman, *The Secret Sayings of Jesus: The Gnostic Gospel of Thomas*, English Translation of the Gospel of Thomas by William R. Schoedel. Doubleday & Company, Inc. 1960, Garden City, New York, p. 186.

Parables

Frame # 25

Given in the exhibit on the opposite page are two parables. Inspect the parables to determine whether they follow the *Subject-Relationship-Enlightening Parallel* order or another order.

1. Write the words *Subject, Relationship, Enlightening Parallel* over the appropriate parts of the parable in # 1.

2. Circle the letter of the statements (below) that describe the parable given in # 2 on the opposite page.

    a. The enlightening parallel stands at the beginning of the parable.

    b. The subject of the parable, which deals with God's relationship to men, stands at the beginning of the parable.

    c. The subject of the parable, which deals with God's relationship to men, stands at the end of the parable.

    d. The words "even so" show a relationship of similarity between the other two parts of the parable.

3. Write the words *Subject, Relationship, Enlightening Parallel* over the appropriate parts of the parable in # 2.

4. Circle the letter of the statement that describes what we have learned about the order in the parables in the exhibit on the opposite page.

    a. The order Subject-Relationship-Enlightening Parallel which is given in # 1 on the opposite page describes *some* parables.

    b. The order Subject-Relationship-Enlightening Parallel which is given in # 1 on the opposite page describes *all* parables.

Parables

ANSWER to Frame # 25

1. Jesus said: The [*Subject*] [*Relationship*] [
   kingdom   is like   a shepherd who had a hundred

   Enlightening Parallel
   sheep. One of them, the largest, lost his way. He left the ninety-nine

   and sought the one until he found it. After he had toiled, he said to

   _____]¹
   the sheep, I love you more than the ninety-nine.

2.
   a, c, d.

3. [
   "Or what woman, having ten silver coins, if she loses one coin, does not

   Enlightening Parallel
   light a lamp and sweep the house and seek diligently until she finds it?

   And when she has found it, she calls together her friends and neighbors,

   _____]
   saying, 'Rejoice with me, for I have found the coin which I had lost.'

   [*Relationship*]   [*Subject*
       Even so,   I tell you, there is joy before the angels of God over one

   _____]
   sinner who repents."   Luke 15:8-10

4.
   a.

Parables

Exhibit for Frame # 26

1. "[Or what woman, having ten silver coins, if she loses one coin, does not light a lamp and sweep the house and seek diligently until she finds it?

   Enlightening Parallel

   And when she has found it, she calls together her friends and neighbors, saying, 'Rejoice with me, for I have found the coin which I had lost.']

   [Relationship]   [**Subject**
   Even so,   I tell you,   there is joy before the angels of God over one sinner who repents.]"

2. "What do you think? A man had two sons; and he went to the first and said, 'Son, go and work in the vineyard today.' And he answered, 'I will not;' but afterward he repented and went. And he went to the second and said the same; and he answered, 'I go, sir,' but did not go. Which of the two did the will of his father?" They said, "The first." Jesus said to them, "Truly, I say to you, the tax collectors and the harlots go into the kingdom of God before you."   Matthew 21:28-31

Parables

Frame # 26

Given in the exhibit on the opposite page are the Parable of the Two Sons and the Parable of the Lost Coin. Note the order of the Parable of the Lost Coin and then determine the order of the Parable of the Two Sons. Is anything missing in the second parable?

1. Cross out the statement that does *not* apply to the Parable of the Two Sons.

   a. The parable begins with the *subject*.

   b. The parable begins with the *enlightening parallel* drawn from everyday life.

   c. The *subject* is separated from the rest of the parable by a question and an answer.

   d. Apparently in the give and take of discussion Jesus omitted words ("like," "even so") which show a *relationship*.

2. Place the words *Subject*, *Relationship*, *Enlightening Parallel* above the parts of the parable that they designate (if such parts are given).

ANSWER to Frame # 26

1.
   a. ~~The parable begins with the *subject*.~~

   b. The parable begins with the *enlightening parallel* drawn from everyday life.

   c. The *subject* is separated from the rest of the parable by a question and answer.

   d. Apparently in the give and take of discussion Jesus omitted words ("like," "even so") which show a *relationship*.

2.

"What do you think? [A man had two sons; and he went to the first and said, 'Son, go and work in the vineyard today.' And he answered, 'I will not;' but afterward he repented and went. And he went to the second and said the same; and he answered, 'I go, sir,' but did not go. Which of the two did the will of his father?" — *Enlightening Parallel*]

They said, "The first." Jesus said to them, ["Truly, I say to you, the tax collectors and the harlots go into the kingdom of God before you." — *Subject*] Matthew 21:28-31

Parables

Frame # 27

Does the parable below contain a subject, words showing a relationship, and an enlightening parallel?

And he said to them, "Which of you who has a friend will go to him at midnight and say to him, 'Friend, lend me three loaves; for a friend of mine has arrived on a journey, and I have nothing to set before him;' and he will answer from within, 'Do not bother me; the door is now shut, and my children are with me in bed; I cannot get up and give you anything?' I tell you, though he will not get up and give him anything because he is his friend, yet because of his importunity he will rise and give him whatever he needs." Luke 11:5-8

Place a check before the responses which make the following statements correct.

1. The parable given above *omits:*

   ___ a. a subject   ___ c. words showing a relationship

   ___ b. an enlightening parallel from everyday life

2. If the parables we have examined in this and previous frames are typical of all parables, we may conclude that the gospel writer always included:

   ___ a. the subject   ___ b. the enlightening parallel from everyday life

   ___ c. words showing a relationship

ANSWER to Frame # 27

1.
   ✓ a. a subject   ✓ c. words showing a relationship

   ___ b. an enlightening parallel from everyday life

2.
   ___ a. the subject   ✓ b. an enlightening parallel from everyday life

   ___ c. words showing a relationship

Note: Sometimes the gospel writer may not have known the subject of a parable. Perhaps at other times he chose not to record it.

Parables

Frame # 28

In this frame you can practice discriminations you have learned. Read the story given below and write the answer to the following questions.

"The kingdom of heaven is like treasure hidden in a field, which a man found and covered up; then in his joy he goes and sells all that he has and buys that field." Matthew 13:44

Write the answers to the following questions.

1. Is the Enlightening Parallel of the above story contrived or artificial? Is it uncontrived, but not ordinary? Give your reasoning below.

_____

_____

2. Does the story tell how life <u>ought to be lived</u> or rather reflect how life <u>actually is lived</u>? Again, write the reasoning for your answer below.

_____

_____

3. Is the above story a parable or allegory? In answering this question point to at least two characteristics of <u>form</u> that helped you to make the identification.

_____

_____

4. Bracket and label with the words *Subject, Relationship, Enlightening Parallel,* the appropriate parts of the story.

Parables

ANSWER to Frame # 28

1. There is nothing contrived or artificial about a Palestinean peasant who unexpectedly finds a treasure in his field, although this is not an everyday occurrence.

   Note: Throughout history conquering armies have swept over Israel and consequently, it became common practice for people to bury their coins. Also, some of the great archaeological discoveries have been made by peasants as they ploughed their fields.

2. The story does not comment on the morality of the peasant's act. We would expect him to look for the owner or perhaps notify the owner of the field.

3. The above story is a parable because there is a relationship of similarity between the subject and the enlightening parallel. Moreover, the enlightening parallel is neither contrived nor artificial, although it is somewhat out-of-the-ordinary.

4. [__Subject__] [Relationship] [_____
   "The kingdom of heaven   is like   treasure hidden in a field,

   _____Enlightening Parallel_____
   which a man found and covered up; then in his joy he goes and sells all

   _____]
   that he has and buys that field."   Matthew 13:44

Parables

Frame # 29

Up to this point you have worked with characteristics of the *form* parable. Now learn to *interpret* the meaning of a given parable. Examine the parable (below) to discover the principle that can be used to interpret it.

["Or what woman, having ten silver coins, if she loses one coin, does not light a lamp and sweep the house and seek diligently until she finds it?

Enlightening Parallel
And when she has found it, she calls together her friends and neighbors, saying, 'Rejoice with me, for I have found the coin which I had lost.']

[*Relationship*] [*Subject*]
Even so, I tell you, there is joy before the angels of God over one sinner who repents." Luke 15:8-10

Circle the letter of the answer which correctly completes the statements given below.

1. First, review the relationship between the subject and the enlightening parallel of a parable.

   a. The subject clarifies or explains the enlightening parallel.
   b. The enlightening parallel clarifies or explains the subject.

Interpretation begins thus with the enlightening parallel from everyday life and moves to God's relationship to men.

2. Thus one principle of interpretation of a parable may be formulated as follows:

   a. as on earth, so in heaven: that is, just as something is true in everyday life, so this same thing is true in terms of God's relationship to men.

   b. as in heaven, so on earth: that is, just as something is true of God's relationship to men, so this same thing is true in everyday life.

ANSWER to Frame # 29

1. b   2. a

Parables

Frame # 30

Use the principle of interpretation - "as on earth, so in heaven" - in order to interpret the Parable of the Lost Coin.

"Or what woman, having ten silver coins, if she loses one coin, does not light a lamp and sweep the house and seek diligently until she finds it? And when she has found it, she calls to-ether her friends and neighbors, saying, 'Rejoice with me, for I have found the coin which I had lost.'

Even so, I tell you, there is joy before the angels of God over one sinner who repents." Luke 15:8-10

Draw a circle around the answers which correctly interpret the above parable.

1. What is true on earth? Examine the *words* of the parable carefully to determine what the enlightening parallel from everyday life is saying.

   a. The story is focusing on the *sadness* of the woman's search.

   b. The story is focusing on the *joy* of the woman who finds a coin after a diligent search.

2. What is true in heaven?

   a. There is joy in heaven when a sinner repents.

   b. There is sorrow in heaven over the sins of a repentant sinner.

3. Now, put the two parts together.

   a. The parable is comparing the woman's sorrow for the lost coin with God's sorrow about men.

   b. The parable is comparing the woman's *joy* in finding the coin with God's *joy* over the sinner who repents.

4. If the above is the correct meaning of the parable, this principle of interpretation has the following implication for finding the meaning of other parables.

   a. The reader should search for the *one point* of comparison the parable makes.

   b. The reader should search for the *hidden subjects* referred to by the key words of the parable. For example, the woman *is* God, the lamp *is* Jesus, and the lost coin *is* lost sinners.

ANSWER to Frame # 30

1.
   a. The story is focusing on the *sadness* of the woman's search.
   b. **(The story is focusing on the *joy* of the woman who finds a coin after a diligent search.)**

2.
   a. **(There is joy in heaven when a sinner repents.)**
   b. There is sorrow in heaven over the sins of a repentant sinner.

3.
   a. The parable is comparing the woman's sorrow for the lost coin with God's sorrow about men.
   b. **(The parable is comparing the woman's *joy* in finding the coin with God's *joy* over the sinner who repents.)**

4.
   a. **(The reader should search for the *one point* of comparison the parable makes.)**
   b. The reader should search for the *hidden subjects* referred to by the key words of the parable. For example, the woman *is* God, the lamp *is* Jesus, and the lost coin *is* lost sinners.

Parables

Exhibit for Frame # 31

[_Subject_][_Relationship_]

1. "Therefore the kingdom of heaven may be compared to a king who wished to settle accounts with his servants. When he began the reckoning, one was brought to him who owed him ten thousand talents; and as he could not pay, his lord ordered him to be sold, with his wife and children and all that he had, and payment to be made. So the servant fell on his knees, imploring him, 'Lord, have patience with me, and I will pay you everything.' And out of pity for him the lord of that servant released him and forgave him the debt. But that same servant, as he went out, came upon one of his fellow servants who owed him a hundred denarii; and seizing him by the throat he said, 'Pay what you owe.' So his fellow servant fell down and besought him, 'Have patience with me, and I will pay you.' He refused and went and put him in prison till he should pay the debt. When his fellow servants saw what had taken place, they were greatly distressed, and they went and reported to their lord all that had taken place. Then his lord summoned him and said to him, 'You wicked servant! I forgave you all that debt because you besought me; and should not you have had mercy on your fellow servant, as I had mercy on you?' And in anger his lord delivered him to the jailers, till he should pay all his debt." Matthew 18:23-34

   Note: The first servant owed a huge debt while the "fellow servant" owed a trifling amount.

2. "For if you forgive men their trespasses, your heavenly Father also will forgive you; but if you do not forgive men their trespasses, neither will your Father forgive your trespasses." Matthew 6:14-15

Parables

Frame # 31

The Parable of the Unmerciful Servant and a teaching about forgiveness are given in the exhibit on the opposite page. Study the exhibit to determine whether the principle of interpretation – "as on earth, so in heaven" – correctly discloses the meaning of the parable.

Cross out those statements which do *not* correctly answer the questions found below.

1. What is true on earth?

    a. While a king forgives servant X a huge debt, servant X refuses to forgive servant Y a trifling amount. Consequently, the king withdraws his forgiveness and sends servant X to jail.

    b. Since servant X cannot possibly pay back the huge debt he owes a king, the king sells servant X and his wife and children to get back as much as possible. Cancelling the debt is not considered.

2. What is true in heaven?

    a. Some aspect of God's relationship to men is illuminated.

    b. This story is contrasting God's attitude toward the forgiveness of sin with that of the earthly king.

3. Put it together.

    a. AS the earthly king refuses to forgive an unforgiving servant, SO there is no forgiveness for an unforgiving person.

    b. AS the earthly king generously forgives an unforgiving servant, SO there is free forgiveness for an unforgiving person.

4. Does the interpretation of the parable agree with the teaching found in Matthew 6:14-15?

    a. The interpretation and the teaching agree.

5. Suppose the parable were really an allegory.

    a. The story yields one point of comparison between the enlightening parallel and God's relationship to men.

    b. The story yields several points of comparison between the enlightening parallel and God's relationship to men: the king *is* God, the debt *is* sin, the jail *is* hell, etc. Indeed if "jail" means hell, the story gives additional instruction about hell. Just as the servant stays in jail until he pays his debts, so men stay in hell until they pay for their sins.

Parables

ANSWER to Frame # 31

1.
   a. While a king forgives servant X a huge debt, servant X refuses to forgive servant Y a trifling amount. Consequently, the king withdraws his forgiveness and sends servant X to jail.
   b. Since servant X cannot possibly pay back the huge debt he owes a king, the king sells servant X and his wife and children to get back as much as possible. Cancelling the debt is not considered.

2.
   a. Some aspect of God's relationship to men is illuminated.
   b. This story is contrasting God's attitude toward the forgiveness of sin with that of the earthly king.

3.
   a. AS the earthly king refuses to forgive an unforgiving servant, SO there is no forgiveness for an unforgiving person.
   b. AS the earthly king generously forgives an unforgiving servant, SO there is free forgiveness for an unforgiving person.

4.
   a. The interpretation and the teaching agree.

5.
   a. The story yields one point of comparison between the enlightening parallel and God's relationship to men.
   b. The story yields several points of comparison between the enlightening parallel and God's relationship to men: the king *is* God, the debt *is* sin, the jail *is* hell, etc. Indeed if "jail" means hell, the story gives additional instruction about hell. Just as the servant stays in jail until he pays his debts, so men stay in hell until they pay for their sins.

Parables

Exhibit for Frame # 32

Parable	Commentary
"For the kingdom of heaven is like a householder who went out early in the morning to hire laborers for his vineyard. After agreeing with the laborers for a denarius a day, he sent them into his vineyard. And going out about the third hour he saw others standing idle in the marketplace; and to them he said, 'You go into the vineyard too, and whatever is right I will give you.' So they went. Going out again about the sixth hour and the ninth hour, he did the same. And about the eleventh hour he went out and found others standing; and he said to them, 'Why do you stand here idle all day?' They said to him, 'Because no one has hired us.' He said to them, 'You go into the vineyard too.' And when evening came, the owner of the vineyard said to his steward, 'Call the laborers and pay them their wages, beginning with the last, up to the first.' And when those hired about the eleventh hour came, each of them received a denarius. Now when the first came, they thought they would receive more; but each of them also received a denarius. And on receiving it they grumbled at the householder, saying, 'These last worked only one hour, and you have made them equal to us who have borne the burden of the day and the scorching heat.' But he replied to one of them, 'Friend, I am doing you no wrong; did you not agree with me for a denarius? Take what belongs to you, and go; I choose to give to this last as I give to you. Am I not allowed to do what I choose with what belongs to me? Or do you begrudge my generosity?" Matthew 20:1-15	A *denarius* was the daily wage for a laborer. It was sufficient for life, but must not be compared with our standard of living. A man could not buy food for his family with the pay for an hour's work.

Parables

Frame # 32

Given in the exhibit on the opposite page is the Parable of the Laborers in the Vineyard. By applying the principle of interpretation - "as on earth, so in heaven" - discover its meaning.

Circle the letter of the statement that correctly interprets the parable.

1. By paying careful attention to the words of the parable determine what the enlightening parallel from everyday life says.

    a. Jesus felt each man should be paid according to his need and told the parable as a critique on the social conditions of his day.

    b. An employer generously pays all his workers the same wage because he has the right to do so, and he wishes to.

2. What does the parable say about the kingdom of heaven; that is, God's rule among men?

    a. Something in the behavior of the householder illumines some aspect of God's dealing with men.

    b. Entrance into the kingdom is determined by good deeds; the more good deeds a person performs, the more likely he is to be invited into the kingdom.

3. What is the meaning of the parable?

    a. Just as the householder acts generously, so God acts generously in his relationships with men.

    b. Just as Jesus felt each man should be paid according to his need, so economic justice will prevail in the kingdom.

ANSWER to Frame # 32

1. b   2. a   3. a

Parables

Frame # 33

Read the rabbinic parable (below) to determine whether the principle of interpretation - "as on earth, so in heaven" - correctly discloses the meaning of the parable.

"The heavens are telling the glory of God."
    Rabbi Ya'akov ben Zabdi said [in explaining the above passage] "This may be compared to a strong man who entered the country and they (the citizens of that country) did not know his strength. A wise man said to them, 'From a stone which he wrestles (lifts) you can observe his strength and his power, so from the heavens we learn the strength of the Holy-One-Blessed-Be-He.'" *Shohar Rob*, page 19.

Note: This famous rabbinic parable was told to explain the verse quoted above it - Psalm 19:1a. Also, it is important to know that the Hebrew word translated glory in Psalm 19:1a comes from the root which means "to be heavy."

Place a check below in the column marked Rabbinic Parable whenever a statement correctly describes that form.

Rabbinic Parable

____   a. As in the parables of Jesus, an enlightening parallel clarifies or explains a subject.

____   b. As in an allegory, a series of key phrases refer to a series of unsignalled subjects.

____   c. If we apply the principle - "as on earth, so in heaven" - we get the meaning: Just as the citizens of a state determine the strength of a stranger by observing how much he can lift, so men determine the power of God by observing the heavens.

____   d. If we allegorize the rabbinic parable we learn that the "strong man" refers to the Devil, the "citizens of that country" refer to people on earth, and the "wise man" refers to God.

____   e. Unlike the parables of Jesus we must allegorize the rabbinic parable before it yields its meaning to us.

____   f. As in the case of the parables of Jesus, the principle - "as on earth, so in heaven" - discloses the meaning of the parable.

ANSWER to Frame # 33

Rabbinic Parable

☑ a. As in the parables of Jesus, an enlightening parallel clarifies or explains a subject.

___ b. As in an allegory, a series of key phrases refer to a series of unsignalled subjects.

☑ c. If we apply the principle - "as on earth, so in heaven" - we get the meaning: Just as the citizens of a state determine the strength of a stranger by observing how much he can lift, so men determine the power of God by observing the heavens.

___ d. If we allegorize the rabbinic parable we learn that the "strong man" refers to the Devil, the "citizens of that country" refer to people on earth, and the "wise man" refers to God.

___ e. Unlike the parables of Jesus we must allegorize the rabbinic parable before it yields its meaning to us.

☑ f. As in the case of the parables of Jesus, the principle - "as on earth, so in heaven" - discloses the meaning of the parable.

Exhibit for Frame # 34

Parable	Commentary
"And he said, 'With what can we compare the kingdom of God,	The kingdom of God is the rule of God in the lives of faithful men. Jesus taught the kingdom was present among his followers. Also, he looked for the coming of the kingdom in its fullness, that is, when all men would acknowledge God as King.
or what parable shall we use for it? It is like	Today, most scholars interpret this as a parable of _contrast_, rather than as a parable of slow growth.
a grain of mustard seed, which, when sown upon the ground, is the smallest of all the seeds on earth; yet when it is sown it grows up and becomes the greatest of all shrubs, and puts forth large branches, so that the birds of the air can make nests in its shade." Mark 4:30-32	

Parables

Frame # 34

Apply the principle of interpretation - "as on earth, so in heaven" - to the Parable of the Mustard Seed, given in the exhibit on the opposite page.

Place a check before the statements below that correctly describe the Parable of the Mustard Seed.

1. What is true on earth?

  ___ a. The parable emphasizes the *contrast* between the tiny seed and the large shrub into which it grows.

  ___ b. The parable emphasizes the *gradual development* of the seed into the large shrub.

2. What is true in heaven?

  ___ a. Faith in the heart of a believer is like a mustard seed: it has a tiny beginning and grows into a large bush.

  ___ b. Presumably the same contrast is true of the kingdom of God. Jesus is contrasting the tiny beginnings of the kingdom in his ministry with its coming great end when God rules over all men as King.

3. What does the parable mean?

  ___ a. The parable compares the gradual development from the tiny seed into the great shrub to the gradual development of the tiny seed of faith in my life into the secure faith of old age.

  ___ b. The parable compares the contrast between the tiny seed and the great shrub to the contrast between the tiny beginnings of God's rule in the lives of a few and its coming great end.

Parables

ANSWER to Frame # 34

1.
- ✓ a. The parable emphasizes the *contrast* between the tiny seed and the large shrub into which it grows.
- ___ b. The parable emphasizes the *gradual development* of the seed into the large shrub.

2.
- ___ a. Faith in the heart of a believer is like a mustard seed: it has a tiny beginning and grows into a large bush.
- ✓ b. Presumably the same contrast is ture of the kingdom of God. Jesus is contrasting the tiny beginnings of the kingdom in his ministry with its coming great end when God rules over all men as King.

3.
- ___ a. The parable compares the gradual development from the tiny seed into the great shrub to the gradual development of the tiny seed of faith in my life into the secure faith of old age.
- ✓ b. The parable compares the contrast between the tiny seed and the great shrub to the contrast between the tiny beginnings of God's rule in the lives of a few and its coming great end.

Parables

Frame # 35

Read the parable given below and interpret it with the help of the questions which are addressed to you.

And he told them a parable: "Look at the fig tree, and all the trees; as soon as they come out in leaf, you see for yourselves and know that the summer is already near. So also, when you see these things taking place, you know that the kingdom of God is near. Luke 21:29-31

Write the answers to the following questions.

1. Make brackets and label each part of the parable with its proper term: *Subject,*
   Relationship,
   Enlightening Parallel.

2. What does the enlightening parallel teach?

_____
_____
_____

3. State the interpretation of the parable.

_____
_____
_____

4. Now write the principle of interpretation that you have followed.

_____

Parables

ANSWER to Frame # 35

1.

And he told them a parable: "Look at the fig tree, and all the trees; as soon as they come out in leaf, you see for yourselves and know that the summer is already near. So also, when you see these things taking place, you know that the kingdom of God is near. Luke 21:29-31

[.... *Enlightening Parallel* ....] [Relationship] [.... Subject ....]

2. The enlightening parallel teaches that one event in nature prepares you for what follows: so the return of foliage to the trees indicates that summer is near.

   Note: If your answer differs substantially from the above, refer back to Frame # 30 and review up to this frame.

3. As the leaves of the trees indicate that summer is near, so "these things" (not stated) indicate that the kingdom of God is near.

4. As on earth, so in heaven.

Parables

Frame # 36

In previous frames we have used the principle of interpretation - "as on earth, so in heaven" - to find the meaning of a parable. Examine the following passage of scripture in order to discover a slightly different version of that principle.

Or what man of you, if his son asks him for a leaf, will give him a stone? Or if he asks for a fish, will give him a serpent? If you then, who are evil, know how to give good gifts to your children, how much more will your Father who is in heaven give good things to those who ask him?
Matthew 7:9-11

Circle the letter of the statement that accurately describes the above passage.

1. What does the passage say?

   a. If evil men know how to give good gifts, we would expect God because of His fatherly goodness also to give good gifts.

   b. If *evil* men know how to give good gifts, *how much more* will God because of His fatherly goodness give good gifts to those who ask Him.

2. What version of the principle of interpretation is found above?

   a. as on earth so in heavenly things

   b. if something is true on earth, how much more is something true of heavenly things

ANSWER to Frame # 36

1. b   2. b

Parables

Exhibit for Frame # 37

(1) He was praying in a certain place, and when he ceased, one of his disciples said to him, "Lord, teach us to pray, as John taught his disciples." (2) And he said to them, "When you pray, say: Father, hallowed be thy name. Thy kingdom come. (3) Give us each day our daily bread; (4) and forgive us our sins, for we ourselves forgive every one who is indebted to us; and lead us not into temptation."

Parable	Commentary
(5) And he said to them, "Which of ycu	The Greek of the phrase "Which of you" is better translated by the following: "Can you imagine that any of you," or "It is unthinkable that any of you..." As the English shows, verses 5-7 are a continuous question.
who has a friend will go to him at midnight and say to him, 'Friend, lend me three loaves; (6)	Three loaves would be a meal for one person.
for a friend of mine has arrived on a journey, and I have nothing to set before him';	Even today it is important to entertain a guest in the Near East.
(7) and he will answer from within, 'Do not bother me; the door is now shut, and my children are with me in bed; I cannot get up and give you anything'?	A wooden or iron bar was drawn through rings attached to the door. Thus opening the door would wake up the whole household who slept together on a raised section of the floor.
(8) I tell you, though he will not get up and give him anything because he is his friend, yet because of his importunity he will rise and give him whatever he needs." Luke 11:1-8	It was unthinkable to refuse such a request for honoring oriental hospitality. If the man will not answer the request on the basis of friendship, he will do it to get rid of the noise.

Parables

Frame # 37

Given in the exhibit on the opposite page is the Parable of the Friend at Midnight, along with the surrounding verses and a commentary. Determine which version of the principle of interpretation best unlocks the meaning of this parable.

Underline the statements that describe the parable.

1. What happens in the enlightening parallel from everyday life?

   a. The friend, because he was a friend, willingly answered the request without protest.

   b. For one reason or another a friend answers his neighbor's midnight request.

2. The gospel suggests that the subject of this parable is prayer. What then is the meaning of the parable?

   a. The principle - "as on earth, so in heaven" - gives this meaning: *as* the friend answers the request, if only to get rid of the inconvenience, *so* God responds to the one who prays, if only to get rid of the inconvenience.

   b. The principle - "if on earth, how much more in heaven" - gives this meaning: *if* the friend answers the request, if only to get rid of the inconvenience, *how much more* (willingly) does God respond to the one who prays.

ANSWER to Frame # 37

1.
   a. The friend, because he was a friend, willingly answered the request without protest.

   b. <u>For one reason or another a friend answers his neighbor's midnight request.</u>

2.
   a. The principle - "as on earth, so in heaven" - gives this meaning: *as* the friend answers the request, if only to get rid of the inconvenience, *so* God responds to the one who prays, if only to get rid of the inconvenience.

   b. <u>The principle - "if on earth, how much more in heaven" - gives this meaning: *if* the friend answers the request, if only to get rid of the inconvenience, *how much more* (willingly) does God respond to the one who prays.</u>

Exhibit for Frame # 38

Parable	Commentary
He said, "In a certain city there was a judge who neither feared God nor regarded man; and there was a widow in that city who kept coming to him and saying, 'Vindicate me against my adversary.'	(The commentary below is a new translation called Today's English Version, published by American Bible Society.) 'Help me against my opponent!'
For a while he refused; but afterward he said to himself, 'Though I neither fear God nor regard man, yet because this widow bothers me, I will vindicate her, or she will wear me out by her continual coming.'"	I will see to it that she gets her rights;
And the Lord said, "Hear what the unrighteous judge says. And will not God vindicate his elect, who cry to him day and night? Will he delay long over them? I tell you, he will vindicate them speedily." Luke 18:2-8	Now, will God not judge in favor of his own people...? ...he will judge in their favor,...

Note: The phrases "vindicate his elect" and "judge in their favor" refer to the Kingdom of God which will come in its fullness at the end of this age (or world). At that time God will set things right in his role as Judge.

Parables

Frame # 38

Read the Parable of the Unjust Judge and the accompanying commentary. Then answer the following questions to determine the meaning of the parable.

Write the answer to the following questions.

1. Bracket, overline, and write the words, *Subject, Enlightening Parallel*, over the appropriate parts of the parable in the exhibit.

2. What is true on earth?

_____
_____

3. What is true in heaven?

_____
_____

Scholars are divided on the meaning of this parable and two interpretations are possible.

a. The principle - "as on earth, so in heaven" - gives this meaning: just as the widow persisted in coming to the unjust judge, so we should persist in coming to God in prayer.

b. The principle - "if on earth, how much more in heaven" - gives this meaning: if an unjust judge finally rules in favor of a widow because of her persistence, how much more speedily will God judge in favor of his people.

4. If we pick interpretation "a" (above), who is the central figure?

_____

5. If we pick interpretation "b" (above), who is the central figure? And what words in the parable itself become important?

_____
_____

6. In view of the above discussion, write the principle of interpretation you would choose in interpreting the parable and show your reasoning.

_____
_____
_____

Parables

ANSWER to Frame # 38

1.
He said, [In a certain city there was a judge who neither feared God nor regarded man; and there was a widow in that city who kept coming to him and saying, 'Vindicate me against my adversary.'   *Enlightening Parallel*   For a while he refused; but afterward he said to himself, 'Though I neither fear God nor regard man, yet because this widow bothers me, I will vindicate her, or she will wear me out by her continual coming.'" And the Lord said, ["Hear what the unrigheous judge says. And will not God vindicate his elect, who cry to him day and night? Will he delay long over them?   *Subject*   I tell you, he will vindicate them speedily."   Luke 18:2-8

2. *An unjust judge finally gives a widow her rights because of her persistence in coming.*

3. *God will speedily judge in favor of his children.*

4. *the widow*   Note: *According to "a" the widow's persistence in coming is compared to our persistence in praying.*

5. *the judge*
he will vindicate them speedily

6. *"if on earth, how much more in heaven" I choose this principle because the "subject" of the parable emphasizes the speed with which God will vindicate his elect. The emphasis of the "subject" does not seem to lie on our persistence. But other authorities disagree.*

Parables

Exhibit for Frame # 39

Parable of the Wheat and the Tares

"The kingdom of heaven may be compared to a man who sowed good seed in his field; but while men were sleeping, his enemy came and sowed weeds among the wheat, and went away. So when the plants came up and bore grain, then the weeds appeared also. And the servants of the householder came and said to him, 'Sir, did you not sow good seed in your field? How then has it weeds?' He said to them, 'An enemy has done this.' The servants said to him, 'Then do you want us to go and gather them?' But he said, 'No; lest in gathering the weeds you root up the wheat along with them. Let both grow together until the harvest; and at harvest time I will tell the reapers, Gather the weeds first and bind them in bundles to be burned, but gather the wheat into my barn.'"   Matthew 13:24-30

An Interpretation

"He who sows the good seed   is   the Son of man;
the field   is   the world,
and the good seed   means the sons of the kingdom;
the weeds   are   the sons of the evil one,
and the enemy who sowed them   is   the devil;
the harvest   is   the close of the age,
and the reapers   are   angels.

Just as the weeds are gathered and burned with fire, so will it be at the close of the age. The Son of man will send his angels, and they will gather out of his kingdom all causes of sin and all evildoers, and throw them into the furnace of fire; there men will weep and gnash their teeth. Then the righteous will shine like the sun in the kingdom of their Father. Matthew 13:37-43a.

Another Interpretation

Apparently Pharisees and others were challenging Jesus to separate out from the mass of people who followed him a pure group who lived by higher standards than the others. In the (above) parable which counseled patience, he said that just as the tares (weeds) are not separated from the wheat until the harvest, so a premature separation of men from the kingdom is to be avoided until the final Judgment.

Parables

Frame # 39

Does the principle of interpretation — "as on earth, so in heaven" produce the same meaning for the parable as the allegorical method of interpretation?

1. Characteristics of the two methods of interpretation are listed below. If a characteristic describes the allegorical method, place a check under the column marked allegorical method. If a characteristic describes the versions of the principle of interpretation that we have been using, place a check under that column.

Principle of Interpretation	Allegorical Method	
___	___	a. There is a relationship of similarity.
___	___	b. There is a relationship of identity.
___	___	c. There are *several* subjects.
___	___	d. There is *one point* of comparison between the enlightening parallel and the subject.
___	___	e. The earthly *is* the heavenly since the story pictures the Last Judgment.
___	___	f. Weeds and wheat in a grain field clarify something in God's relationship to men.

2. Place a check before the statement which describes what the **allegory** teaches.

   ___ a. The story contrasts the fate of evildoers and the righteous in the Last Judgement.

   ___ b. The story counsels patience lest *men* attempt to decide who is in the kingdom of heaven and who is to be cast out.

3. Now check the answer which correctly describes the relationship of the allegorical method of interpretation to this parable.

   The allegorical method ___ a. arrives at the same meaning for the parable as the principle "as on earth, so in heaven."

   ___ b. changes and distorts the meaning of the parable.

Parables

ANSWER to Frame # 39

1.

Principle of Interpretation	Allegorical Method	
✓	—	a. There is a relationship of similarity.
—	✓	b. There is a relationship of identity.
—	✓	c. There are *several* subjects.
✓	—	d. There is *one point* of comparison between the enlightening parallel and the subject.
—	✓	e. The earthly *is* the heavenly since the story pictures the Last Judgment.
✓	—	f. Weeds and wheat in a grain field clarify something in God's relationship to men.

2.

✓ a. The story contrasts the fate of evildoers and the righteous in the Last Judgement.

___ b. The story counsels patience lest *men* attempt to decide who is in the kingdom of heaven and who is to be cast out.

3.

The allegorical method ___ a. arrives at the same meaning for the parable as the principle "as on earth, so in heaven."

✓ b. changes and distorts the meaning of the parable.